D0777182

Love Poems

by

Purple Ronnie

Also by Purple Ronnie

Purple Ronnie's Book of Love

☆

Purple Ronnie's Guide to Life

☆

The Smashing World of Purple Ronnie

☆

Purple Ronnie's Star Signs

Published in 1994 by Statics(London) Ltd
41 Standard Road, London NW10 6HF
Tel: 081-965 3327

© 1994 Giles Andreae

ISBN 1-873922-28-0

Print origination by Diva Graphics

Printed in England by H·P·H Print Ltd
Unit 3, Royal London Estate, 29 North Acton Road
London NW10 6PE

Words by : Giles Andreae

Pictures by : Janet Cronin
and Giles Andreae

additional material: Simon Andreae

To my mates

Nev, Maisie, Gordon and Shirlee

Contents

loads of
soppy love poems
by <u>me</u>

a poem about
↓

Loving You

How many ways do I love you?

I think there are probably two

The rumpety-pump way

Is all very well

But I like the soppy way too

Kissing

teeny peck →

Some kisses last for just seconds
They're gentle and go on the cheeks
But I like the ones you put
right on the lips
That can go on for 2 or 3 weeks

scrumptious

massive snog →

tick tick

...604812 seconds
604813 seconds

Smashing Mate

You're chocolate cake
and soft ice-cream
Piled high upon my plate
You're a double jelly
Sandwich dream
My splendid smashing mate

a poem to say

I Love You

Sometimes when it's late at night
And we're alone together
I want to take you in my arms
And cuddle you for ever

Love

Love,
When we're <u>SNOGGING</u>
I'd like to crumble
Biscuits in your hair

Friends

Some people think that it's great
to be rich
To be cool and keep up with the
trends
But riches and looks just don't
matter at all
Cos what really counts is your friends

no
cash
↓

smashing
mates →

← Nev's
latest
tie

a poem about ↓

Sex Maniacs

They dream about sex every hour
of the day
They dream when they work
And they dream when they play
They dream about sex in the bath
and in bed
They never get naughty thoughts
out of their head

a poem about a ↓

Huggle

A huggle is something you share
with a friend
You can huggle in all kinds of ways
Huggling makes you feel all sort
of warm
And perfectly splendid for days

us after
a good
huggle

a poem for a

Gorgeously Smashing
Person

However much money I pay people

Some of them still won't agree

That you're almost as

wonderfully scrumptious

And gorgeously smashing as me

mirror

us looking
gorgeously
smashing

How to Be a Boyfriend

Sometimes you've got to be macho

And do lots of things that are tough

But sometimes it's best to be quiet and gentle

And say loads of soppy type stuff

whisper

It's good to have hundreds of muscles

And girls always like a nice bum

But you mustn't be hairy or sweaty

Or have any flab on your tum

or fat

Don't ever talk about football
Or make nasty smells in the bed
Or joke about bosoms with mates in
the pub
Or drink till you're out of your head

You've got to be funny and clever
And do loads of things by surprise
Like shouting out loud in the back of
the bus
"My girlfriend's got beautiful eyes!"

You don't need to have too much money
But make sure you've just got enough
To buy loads of presents and chocolates
                                and flowers
And sexy silk undies and stuff

Say to your girlfriend "you're gorgeous
Your body's a twelve out of ten
You're sexy and beautiful, clever and kind"
Then tell her all over again

Blah Blah

what a super boyfriend

CHOCS

a poem about

Missing You

There are times when I really
do miss you
And think of you missing me too
So I close my eyes tight
And I daydream
That I am together with you

Snogging

It's funny how us people
Show our love by touching tongues

But at least we're not all doggies

Or we'd sniff each others <u>bums!</u>

My Lover

bestest friends

I'd like to tell you something
I hope it won't offend
But if you weren't my lover
You'd be my bestest friend

us wearing
saucy
undies

a poem about ↓

My Friend

A friend is a person who helps
you to laugh
And makes you feel happy and free
A friend is the grooviest thing
you can have
A friend is what <u>You</u> are to ME

a recipe for ↓

Love Pie

by Purple Ronnie

Take a pint of tickle juice
And whisk it till it's thick
Pick a crop of cuddle fruit
And crush them with a stick

hee
hee
hee
hee

Nibble eighteen earlobes
As gently as you can
Then grate a little botty kiss
And put it in the pan

Dip a snog in snuggle sauce
And let it rest a while
Then soak it in hug marinade
And season with a smile

Add a pinch of happy spice
Brown in huggle town
And bake it in the oven
Till it comes out golden brown

a poem about

cuddling

I sometimes have feelings
You don't understand
That make me confused and befuddled
So don't go to sleep
When you turn out the light
Cos sometimes I like to be cuddled

a poem for a
↓

Loving Person

Loving people like to give
Their love to everyone
That's why Loving People's love
Is so much lovely fun

a shy poem
↓
To Someone I Like

I sometimes find it rather hard

To say I really care

And that I like you quite a lot

But I've said it now - so there

hot
flush

a poem about

↓

Love

Sometimes it makes you feel happy
And sometimes it makes you feel blue
But I find it makes me feel smashingly
Fab
And that's cos I'm in it with YOU

Men

Some men I know
Make love into an art
And always keep going
Till morning
But others I know
Just roll over and fart
When they've finished the job
Then start snoring

Love Poem

I just want to tell you
I love you so much
That each time I look at your face
My heart jumps a somersault
Round in the air
And my feelings explode into space

a poem about feeling

Smiley Inside

Love makes you feel all cuddly
and warm

Love makes your tongue get all tied

It makes you go wobbly

And weak at the knees

And all sort of smiley inside

I Like You

You tell me I'm fat and I'm ugly

You tell me I'm utterly nuts

You tell me I burp and I fart
and I smell

But that's why I like you so
much

Snuggly Poem

I'd like to be a hamster

Or a hedgehog or a shrew

And go into my hidey hole

To snuggle up with you

Doing It

Who first thought of doing
What it is you're meant to do?
I'm glad he was so brainy
I'd have never guessed would you?

a poem for a
↓

Lover

If someone invented a gadget
That made me terrific in bed
I think I'd buy twenty-five thousand
And Do It with you till I'm dead

a poem to say

I Love You

When I am lying alone in my bed
All sorts of thoughts come into my head
Like why do I Love You as much as I do?
Then I know it's because you are You

My Own Little Way

I sometimes get rather embarrassed
And don't always know what to say
When it comes to expressing my
feelings

But I try in my own little way

a poem about

Men I Like

I like men who talk
About interesting things
Like music and science and art
But most men I know
When they've had a few drinks
Just talk about sex and then fart

a soppy
Love Poem

Crikey I love you to pieces
My heart wants to jump up and shout
Let's walk through the flowers
And huggle for hours
And let all our loveliness out

Snuggle Pie

You to me are everything
That money just can't buy

Like creamy cuddle custard
And scrumptious snuggle pie

custard love

a poem for an

Extra Special Friend

If I had a million pounds
I know what I would do
I'd buy some extra special times
And spend them all with you

Hugging Poem

I want you to know
That I think you are great
And although I'm a bit of a mug
If you ever need me
I'll always be near
To come round and give you a

hug

squeeze

feeling → better

Being in Love

thumpety thump

Whenever I'm with you
My heart starts to thump
And I come over wonky and flustered
I try to stay calm
But pour milk on my toast
And butter my coffee with mustard

me so
in Love

MILK

a poem for a

B O Y F R I E N D

You're a hunky handsome
heart-throb
You're a fab and groovy dude
You're a juicy lump of
gorgeousness
A scrumptious plate of food

Loving

Loving a person is easy
If only you've got the right knack
—It's heaping your happiness
All over someone
Who loves heaping happiness back

What is Love?

It must be sort of squidgey
Like a bouncy rubber ball
Cos I know that when you fall
                    in it
It doesn't hurt at all

I know that people make it
But they never tell me where
And I think that there's a funny tribe
Who rub it in their hair

love
dance

piece
of
love

I wonder what
      it looks like
I've heard it's splendid stuff
I suppose it's sort of furry
Like my tummy button fluff